DIVINE TIE D
Made in Minutes

For Ages 8 to 80

This book is to help teach anyone

interested in making beautiful tie dyes,

how to make them easily every time,

in just a few minutes.

TK

Trinity Kellner

Dedication

This book is gratefully dedicated to God –

Who makes all things possible.

Divine (di - vin')

1. Of God.

2. Supremely good.

Tie - dye

Way of dyeing cloth in patterns by tying sections tightly so they will not absorb dye.

Acknowledgments

I would like to thank the following people for their unconditional love and support:

My wonderful, multi-talented teenagers Melissa Santana Rose and Michael Darrenger; my kind, flower-children parents, Watwi and Banana; my beautiful friends, Angie Michele Garmisa, Tricia Lynn Pilkington, Heidi Lee Harter, Rachel Mary Kemble Torrey, Regina LeAnn Cox, and Mary Pauline Morse. I would also like to thank Dharma Trading Co. for their excellent products and service and the Grateful Dead for the inspiration.

~ Mahalo ~

Table of Contents

Introduction

1986. I was 15 years old at my first Grateful Dead concert. The tie dyed tapestries and shirts I saw were so colorful and psychedelic; seeing them gave me the inspiration to become a tie-dyer and make tie-dyes that good.

When I returned home to Idyllwild, California, I began making tie dyes - not having a clue as to what I was doing. Yet, after many years of learning by doing and a lot of practice, I make them now with ease in just a few minutes. In this "how to" book, I will share with you what works best for me and how I make them.

Happy Tie Dye'in! –T

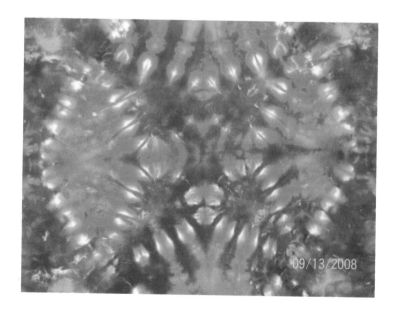

Poem
By Watwi

Take a piece of cotton

White is usually best

Buy your dyes from Dharma

In supplies, invest.

You will need a work-space

Rubber bands and gloves

Bottles, dyes, soda-ash

Water and some love.

With imagination

Tie dyes can be made

With colorful designs

Artfully displayed.

(April '09)

*"Everything that is really great and inspiring is created by the
individual who can labor in freedom."*
Albert Einstein – Physicist

Tools and Mixing

First thing I do is put some bootleg Grateful Dead on the stereo (it's best to tie and dye outside). I like to use a big glass table to do my tying on and I use a 25-gallon plastic tub full of plain water to get my items wet then wring them out and place them on the table to tie.

1-800-542-5227 is the number for Dharma Trading Company in San Rafael, CA. I've been dealing with them for 22 years and they are most excellent in their products and their service. In my opinion, they're #1 in their field. They supply everything you'll need to make tie dyes.

For Tying I always be sure to have these items on hand: rubber bands, artificial sinew, scissors, yardstick, ruler, cloth tape measure, Crayola washable markers – 1 with a 3 or 4 foot string tied to it to be used as a compass.

For Pre-Soak After having tied a few items, I use another large plastic tub. I use a 5-gallon plastic Sparkletts bottle so the solution becomes completely mixed. It's one cup of soda ash (sodium carbonate) per gallon of hot water. Allow your items to soak for at least 15 minutes and become saturated; reuse solution until gone.

Soda ash is essential as it is the key that locks the dye into the fabric. When I remove the items, I squeeze out excess solution and place on clean plastic grills to be dyed.

When I mix dye, I like to have the following on hand: rubber gloves, dust mask, eye protection, purified warm water (hot for turquoise), non-iodized salt (1 tbsp. per each 8 ounce of liquid dye – only black). I mix new black with better black with the salt for the darkest black. A tbsp. measuring container, measuring cups, 32 oz. squeeze bottles, funnel, urea (optional).

Mix the dye in a well-ventilated area – outside is ideal. Colors with no star on the container require 2 tsp. per 8 oz. (cup) of warm water, 1 star – I use 3 tsp. and 2 stars (blacks) require 4 tsp. per cup. I like to mix about 14 cups of dye at a time, so I convert the tsp. to tbsp. (saves time).

Spiral

The spiral was the first design I ever made and probably the easiest, although, in my opinion, all of the designs are easy, once you know how to make them. I will do my best to explain to you in this book in the most simplified terms possible, the easiest way to produce the designs you desire. The first thing to do is get the fabric thoroughly wet, wring out, shake out, then place the front face down on the glass. I then determine where I want the center of the spiral to be (I usually use the center of the fabric). I pinch the material at that spot and keeping my fingertips pressed firmly against the table, I begin turning the material in a clockwise fashion. The material will automatically start pleating in a circular fashion and I keep those pleats or folds all the same size. I continue turning the fabric until it looks like this:

Then I use 4 rubber bands to hold it together so it looks like this:

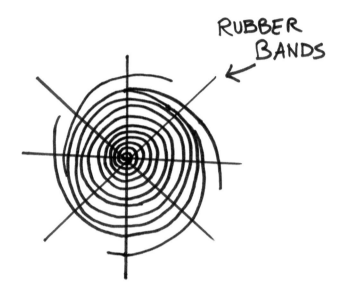

Then it goes into the pre-soak solution for at least 15 minutes so it becomes completely saturated. After that, with rubber gloves on, I remove it from the pre-soak and squeeze out the excess solution leaving it damp and placing it on a clean plastic grill. Now it's ready to dye. The front of the spiral is facing up so it is the first side to be dyed. Using the squeeze bottles, I put the colors I want to use on it like it's a pie and each color is a pie piece, overlapping the edges creating new colors if you choose to do so. I sometimes use the rubber bands as guides.

I use enough dye to penetrate the material. When I'm done dyeing the front side, I let it sit for a few minutes before flipping it over onto a clean part of the grill and I usually put the same colors in the same places. Sometimes, I'll use the same colors in the same order, only moved over 1.

Example: Deep orange goes where the fire red is, fire red where the bright yellow is and so on and so forth. There are so many different ways to do it, it's incredible. Whatever you decide, it'll still come out unique and created by you. I personally like to cover the entire spiral with turquoise, then cover with fuchsia red, then a little more turquoise and do the same on the other side and it makes a beautiful purple-violet, outlined by turquoise. Nice!

4 Spirals

Fold the piece to by dyed (for this design, I like to use a 100% cotton sheet) in half one way and in half the other way, so the front is on the inside of the folds. Then I tie it the same way as the spiral. Dyeing it in pie pieces works great; if you like, you can also do pie pieces inside of pie pieces inside of pie pieces. After dyeing an item, I put it on clean, dry rags in the sun, then cover with plastic as this helps the colors to explode. Overnight is best to let them sit.

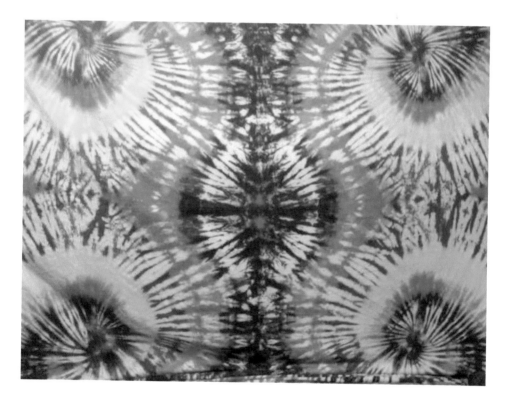

Heart

When I make a heart on a tapestry, I like it to be perfectly centered when it's finished. To make it like that, I take my damp 100% cotton material and fold it in half (front on inside of fold) (#1). Then fold it in half the other way to determine where the center is and make a mark with a washable marker (#2). Fold it once more the same way to find the midway point between the center and the edge; make a mark (#3). Unfold it so it looks like #1, except now you have 3 marks on it. From the top mark, I draw a line parallel with the edge (#4). Then I draw half of a heart (#5). Starting at either end of the line, I fan-fold (pleat) the material all the way up the line to the other end keeping the folds all the same size and making the line straight. Holding the material tightly together with my fingers, I place a rubber band over the line making it very tight (#6). If I want a wider border around the heart, then I simply add more rubber bands tightly next to that one. With the rest of the material, I usually crunch it up and rubber band it (not tightly) so it stays together when I flip it over. I put it in the pre-soak for at least 15 minutes; then when I'm dyeing it, I remember which section is the heart and usually dye it fire red (both sides) or turquoise and fuchsia red. The rest of it, I pretty much use whatever color appeals to me at the time. Applying them in bands or zigzags or whatever. Sometimes, I'll put bands of, say, green, turquoise, deep orange, bright yellow, then scatter black over it (not the heart) leaving only a little color showing. Repeat on other side and the finished product looks super psychedelic!

4 Hearts

This is a pretty cool design to put on tapestries. I fold the material in fourths, so it resembles #2 (previous page), then using a ruler and washable marker, I draw on it to look like #7. After that I fan-fold all the lines and rubber-band them (3 lines) so it now looks like #8. I measure everything, so the finished product looks professional. The center becomes a diamond which I usually crunch real tight or spiral or fan-fold it from the corner, which is the center to make it look like the ripple. When I dye the item, I use whatever colors stimulate my senses at the time, knowing where the hearts are and dyeing them a complimentary color such as red, purple or pink. I usually crunch around the hearts and diamond and rubber band like before when we did the heart and spiral(s).

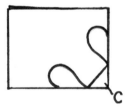

C

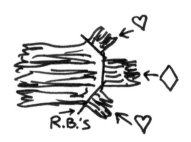

R.B.'s

Crunch

The crunch designs are probably my favorite because if they're done correctly with the right amount of dye and mixtures of colors, the designs and faces, etc. that show up in the finished product are awesome. If I'm making a shirt, I first turn it inside out, get it wet, wring out, shake out and place on table, front face down. (#1) I scrunch it up making as many folds and wrinkles as possible. (#2) Then I put rubber bands around it (not tight), just enough to keep it from falling apart or taco-ing when I flip it over when dyeing it. (#3) When dyeing it, I just use my imagination and I like to put many different colors on it (both sides) using a lot of dye, but not too much. This one takes a little more practice than others and when you master it, you'll see why it's a favorite. Sometimes, I fold it in half first (#4) with the front on the inside of the fold – then scrunch it (#2) and band it (#3) for a different effect.

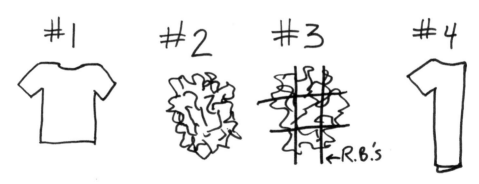

V-Fold

Otherwise known as the "rib-cage" design. This one is fairly easy and comes out looking nice. Although, there are a few variations to it, they basically all consist of pleating and scrunching. I begin with a damp, new shirt and fold it in half with the front on the inside of the fold (as I want the front to look the best). Then I start pleating it going from A to B, keeping the folds small and all the same size. I then rubber-band it semi-tight to keep it together. Section C, I scrunch and band-like a normal "crunch". When dyeing it, I put colors on it that look good together. An example is the "chakra" colors... red, orange, yellow, green, turquoise, blue, then a beautiful indigo/violet at the top. One of the many cool things about making tie dyes is there are so many different ways to make them, they all come out beautiful and unique made by you.

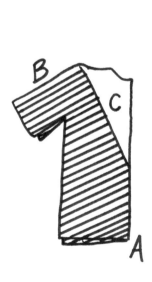

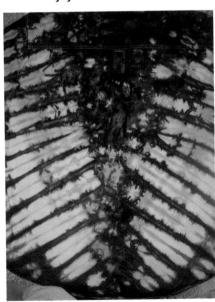

Bandoleer

This is another easy to make design which comes out looking good on a shirt. First, I take a new, damp shirt and lay it out flat on the table (front side facing up). Then I pleat it from A to B. Once that is done, I use 3 rubber bands to bind that section semi-tight. I then crunch sections C and D and band it just enough to keep it together. When dyeing it, I use the same colors on C and D. For the bandoleer, I usually do a band of red, a band of yellow and a band of green. Whatever colors you choose to use, it will still come out looking great.

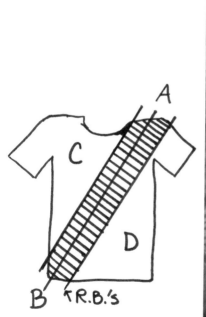

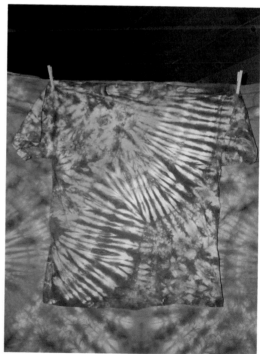

Ripple

We like to call this design the "Ripple" because the finished product looks like a pool of water someone tossed a stone into causing it to ripple out like sound waves. I start with a new, camp shirt and fold it evenly into fourths with the front on the inside of the folds. Fan-folding it just like the previous designs, I connect A to B and rubber band it so as to keep it together. This particular design requires a little more dye than usual as it's thicker from being in fourths. With a little practice, it will look just like I described it above.

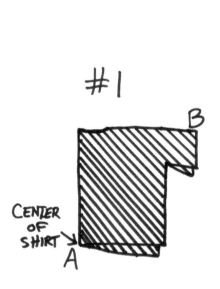

Tribal Necklace

Here is another easy to make design for a t-shirt that comes out looking great. I start with a new, damp shirt and fold it evenly in half with the front on the inside (#1). Starting at the shoulder, A, I pleat it to connect with B, curving it slightly. I then rubber band that section tightly. C and D, I crunch and dye C the same as D. With a little practice, your shirt will look like you're wearing a necklace made of bone.

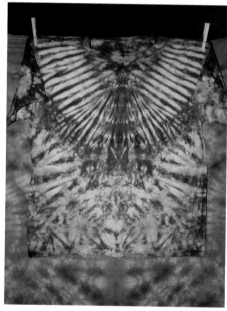

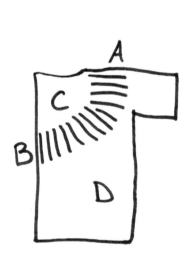

Sun

This is an easy to make, awesome design for a tapestry. I start with a damp 100% cotton duck hanging or sheet and fold it into fourths with the front on the inside (#1). Then I connect A to B so it looks like (#2). I flip it over and do the same so now it looks like (#3). I then take my washable marker/compass and draw an arc from the center (C), keeping it an equal distance on each side (this will be the sun). Then I measure out from the sun the same distance and on each side draw half of a drop (flame) making them the same size (#4). I do different variations with this pattern such as: I alternate the flames (drops) (#5) or I make the flames face the other direction (#6) or I alternate them, making one side longer (#7).

Anyway, it's done. It will come out looking great. I start at one end of the arc (the sun) and pleat the material along the entire length of the line keeping the line straight. Then with rubber bands or artificial sinew, I secure it tightly along the line. Then I crunch or ripple the sun and band it so it stays together (not tight). Then I pleat each flame (drop), making the lines straight and securing it tightly. Crunching the rest of the material and securing it loosely with rubber bands completes the tying phase of this project. I dye the sun and flames the same colors, e.g., red, orange, yellow – and the rest of the material, I'll do like turquoise, blue-violet, and black. The contrast is killer.

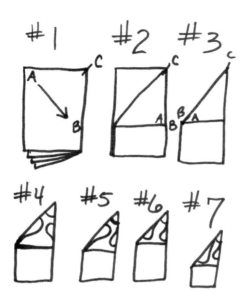

Mandala

Here is another easy to make design for a tapestry that can be done a number of ways. I fold my damp material so it looks like diagram (#3), previous design (Sun). With a washable marker, I draw lines on it so it looks like (#1), or something similar. Starting at the shortest line next to the center (C), I pleat each line, one at a time, making the line straight, then binding it tightly with sinew or rubber bands making it look something like (#2). When dyeing this particular design, I like to have the colors I'm using on it mixes 1/2 strength (1/2 dye and 1/2 warm purified water) and full strength (except black). Here's an example on applying the colors: A – Strong blue-violet, B –1/2 strength blue-violet, C – Strong turquoise, D – 1/2 strength turquoise, E – Strong black, F – ½ strength turquoise, G – Strong turquoise, H – 1/2 strength blue-violet, I – Strong blue violet. Repeat on the other side the same way. The finished tapestry now has depth (from the shades) and looks 3-dimensional.

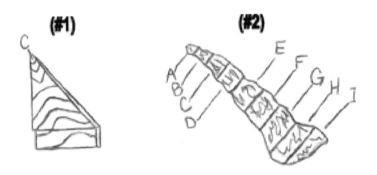

Peace Sign

This design took me a long time to figure out. Once you know how to do it though, you'll find that it is easy like the others. So, here's how you do it: First, I fold my damp material in half (front on inside), and find and mark the center (#1). Then I fold it so A connects to B and C with D so now it looks like (#2). Using my compass (string/washable marker), I draw an arc from the center from side to side reaching almost to the edge. I decide how wide I want the peace sign, say 8", then I measure 8" from each end of the arc toward the center. Then I draw another arc connecting the two 8" marks creating an arc parallel to the outer one. Where the two edges meet (Z), I measure 4" from each edge and draw two lines parallel to the edges (#2). I then pleat it from the center, connecting a to b, making that line straight and banding it tightly along the line with either rubber bands or sinew. Ten I connect c to d and do the same thing. Then I connect e to f, pleating it the entire way, making that line straight and banding it tightly. With the rest of the material (sections i and j), I crunch it and band it enough to keep it together. It should now look something like (#3). When dyeing it, if I use all the same colors on g, h, I, and j, then the peace sign totally different colors, it will appear to be a floating peace sign.

(#1) **(#2)** **(#3)**

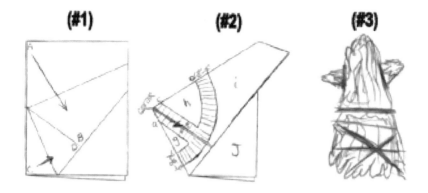

Floating Peace Sign Front   **& Back**

Rinsing, Washing Out

First, I pre-fill a washing machine with hot water and add 1/4 cup of Synthropol or another approved textile detergent. The special detergent is essential as it keeps the colors suspended in animation and keeps the white areas white – hence, no bleeding or running.

I cut the rubber bands off and put 6 shirts or 2 tapestries in the washer and run it through a full cycle. (Don't put too many items in at once or they will get muddy.) When they are done, I like to hang them out on a clothesline to dry so I can see what I created and grade them accordingly, taking pictures of the good ones. The ones that aren't so good, I'll know what to do different next time. Because it's all about learning and no matter how good I think I made an item, there can always be room for improvement so they become divine.

Afterthoughts

Thank you for purchasing and reading this book. I hope it is easy to understand and that it helps to guide you on your psychedelic tie dye journey. There are countless other designs and patterns to learn and master. From what I know, the ancient early Egyptians were the first humans to actually discover and produce "tie dyes." I feel fortunate to be involved in an art form dating back thousands of years. Tie dyes are always beautiful, always unique, and they always bring smiles and happiness to the recipients of said items. With that said, good luck, God bless, and have fun!

Peace, Love, and Harmony,

Trinity Kellner

Poem
By Watwi

African art
made popular by hippies
now worn by babies
businessmen
housewives
students
anyone.
Tie dyes reflect
the universal love for
colorful designs
in clothing
curtains
bedspreads
tapestries.
You can make them
with a few supplies, lots of
imagination
and this book
which tells
each step
to follow.
Wear them with pride
and hang them over windows
decorate your room
give some away
sell them
or keep
forever.

(April '09)

Tie Dyes
By Watwi

Wear a rainbow
　　Hang it high
　　　　Every color
　　　　　　In tie dyes.

This book tells you
　　How to start
　　　　Mr. Kellner
　　　　　　Knows his art.

Dye a t-shirt
　　and some pants
　　　　　　Or maybe skirt
　　　　　　　　For the dance.

A tapestry
　　any size
　　　　on bed or wall
　　　　　　Pleases eyes.

On your windows
　　Curtains too

With sunlight
Shining through.
Get some cotton
It's the best
Some rubber bands
Mix and test.
Purple, yellow
Green and glue
Turquoise, red and
Black works too.
Learn the crunches
Folds and ties
Invest designs
Nice surprise.
From Africa
Tie dyes came
Then the hippies
Brought them fame.
Universal
and unique
Make a statement:
Hand-made chic.
You can wear them
And display
Even sell or
Give away.
With some practice
You will be
Artistic like
Trinity.

(April '09)

To Dye For
By Watwi

My sheets and towels
All clean and white
hung on the line
and caught his sight.
My son said, "Mom!
I'd better dye
those white things there
and you'll see why."
Soon every scrap
of cotton white
was colorful
and nicely bright.
Now twenty years
have passed us by
and Trinity
still makes tie dyes.

(April '09)

CPSIA information can be obtained
at www.ICGtesting.com
Printed in the USA
LVIW021459080712

289213LV00007B

9 781452 806112